I Am

Annie Giang

Ink & Thoughts—Houston, TX
ISBN: 979-8-218-36913-2
Library of Congress Control Number: 2024903272
Title: *I Am*
Author: Annie Giang
Paperback | 2024

Disclaimer:

This journal is not intended as a substitute for medical advice nor a diagnosis from a licensed professional. Always seek the advice of a qualified mental health professional or other healthcare provider for any questions you have regarding your mental health.

This journal belongs to:

____

INDEX

PERSONAL DEVELOPMENT GOALS:

Please understand this: Bad chapters can still create great stories. Wrong paths can still lead to right places. Failed dreams can still create successful people. Sometimes it takes losing yourself to find yourself.

CAREER GOALS:

Plant yourself where your humanity is valued. Not just where your usefulness is valued. You're a human being not a human resource.

HEALTH GOALS:

Be patient with yourself, even when you've let yourself down for the 100th time. No one's out here just making perfect progress. Everyone you admire has let themselves down hundreds of times, too. Just keep going.

MENTAL HEALTH GOALS:

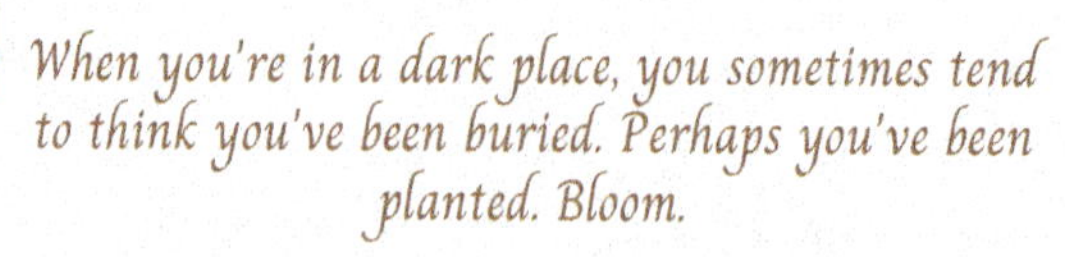

When you're in a dark place, you sometimes tend to think you've been buried. Perhaps you've been planted. Bloom.

WHAT I LOVE ABOUT MYSELF:

WHAT I CAN DO TO HELP OTHERS:

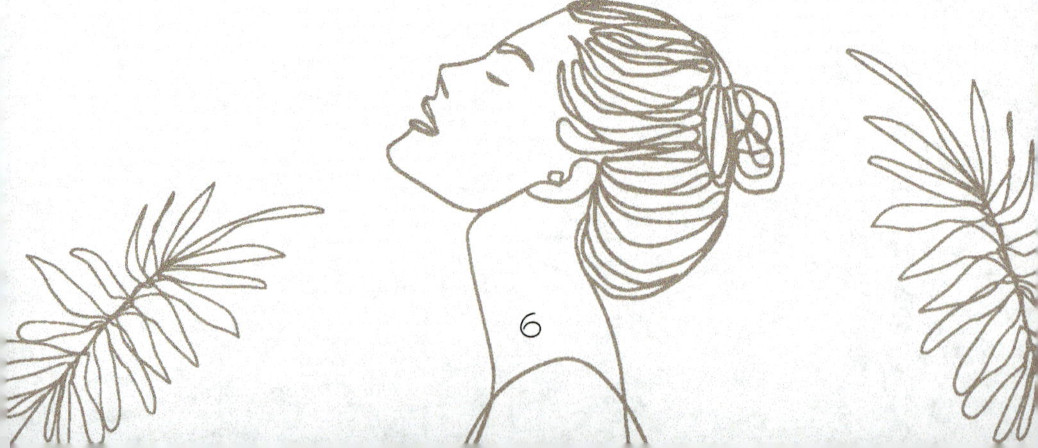

In case you need to hear this.

The woman you're becoming will cost you people, relationships, spaces and material things. Choose her over everything.

It's okay to be kind without expecting kindness in return.

Be careful not to make healing your entire identity. The ego is always searching for neat, definable labels to attach itself to. Make sure you define yourself by living, experiencing, being. You aren't a problem that needs to be solved.

There is nothing wrong with you. You have patterns to unlearn, new behaviors to embody and wounds to heal. You are unlearning generations of harm and remembering love. It takes time.

What is coming is better than what is gone.

Daily Journal

Date ______________

Daily Journal

Date ______________________

Believe in yourself. ______________________

Daily Journal

Date ________

Daily Journal

Date ________

Start with the thing that is small, that you can control.

Daily Journal

Date ______

Daily Journal

Date ______________

You're not broken.
You're healing.

Daily Journal

Date ________

Write a letter of forgiveness to someone
who caused you pain, including yourself.

Affirm: My life is amazing. Everything is going to workout as it should. Everything I am going through is making way for the blessings I have been manifesting. I believe that good things will come unexpectedly.

Daily Journal

Date ___________

*Someone out there feels
better because you exist.*

Daily Journal

Date ________________

Daily Journal

Date ______________

I hope you speak a little
more kindly to yourself
today.

The next stage of your life will require you to be perceived. And to be perceived wrongly. Where your journey is taking you will require you to be okay with it.

Daily Journal

Date ______________

Daily Journal

Date ____________________

Go laugh in places you've cried. Change the narrative.

Daily Journal

Date ___________

Daily Journal

Date ___________

I'm sorry if someone broke your heart and the healing process is still taking a toll, if they made you feel like you're hard to love, or if they didn't handle yours with care. Know that this feeling doesn't last forever. One day, you'll look back and wonder why you ever worried.

Daily Journal   Date ―――――

The walls you build to keep the pain away will
be the same reason that keep people who want
to love you away.

How did your darkest moments shape you
into who you are today?

In case you need to hear this.

You should be proud of yourself for deciding your story
is so much more than the limits of it's past chapters.

You should be proud of yourself for deciding you're worthy of
being loved even while you learn to love yourself.

You should be proud of yourself for finding your strength
again after life made you doubt it existed.

You should be proud of yourself for finding love within
yourself after someone made you feel unworthy.

Daily Journal

Date ____________

Daily Journal

Date ____________

Date ____________

Daily Journal

Date ______________

Decline the small lover. Keep declining it. You deserve a connection where you're both deeply committed to providing emotional responsiveness and mutual care.

Daily Journal

Date ______________

Daily Journal

Date ______________

Daily Journal

Date _____________

Rest your heart and pace
yourself. What will be, will be.
Let it all unfold. Be patient
with yourself and enjoy the
journey for what it is. Love
yourself and love others.
Just rest, keep resting.

Daily Journal

Date ___________

Daily Journal

Date _______________

Daily Journal

Date ___________

Our time is finite here. Be intentional with your heart.

Daily Journal

Date ______________

Daily Journal

Date ______________

Keep going. Don't worry about all the moving parts. Focus on what you need to get from point A to point B. Problem solve from there and get to point C. Solutions appear along the way, because you keep going, problem-solving, and trusting the process. The resources and divine support you need are aligning for you. Don't give up.

What are some boundaries your
future self will enforce?

Daily Journal

Date ___________

Daily Journal

Date ___________

Daily Journal

Date ___________

In case you need to hear this.

Learn how to work with what you have by embracing all that you are. In order to love who you are, you can't hate any versions of yourself that got you to where you are. Heal your trauma so you can name things, release the shame, you keep refining yourself. You keep going.

Don't think about what can happen in a month. Don't think about what can happen in a year. Just focus on the 24 hours in front of you and do what you can to get closer to where you want to be.

Some of your life's best days haven't event happened yet. You have not see it all. You have not felt it all. There are more people for you to meet, places to see and "firsts" to experience.

Daily Journal

Date ___________

Daily Journal

Date _______________

Forgive yourself for the stagnancy that was produced from your depression.

Daily Journal

Date ___________

Don't compare your Chapter 1 to someone else's Chapter 20.

Daily Journal

Date ___________

A heart that's in alignment will give you reciprocity. It understands the value you bring and wants to add value to you. If you feel like an experience is depriving you of what you need, maybe you're "working too hard" for a heart that's not in alignment.

Daily Journal

Date ____________

It's all gonna work out. Trust the process.

Daily Journal

Date __________

Date _____________

All you can do is all you can do.
Focus on what you can control, relate
what you can't.

If you focus on the hurt, you will continue to suffer. If you focus on the lesson, you will continue to grow. Know the power of your mind and program it for success. You have the power within you to overcome every situation. Realize this, and you will find strength.

Daily Journal

Date ______________

Daily Journal

Date _______________

Be someone you love, first.

Daily Journal

Date ___________

Daily Journal

Date ____________

Stay operating out of love instead of fear as much as possible, even when your ego says not to.

The simplest way to stop yourself from
falling back into old cycles and habits
when you move to a new space, is
telling yourself, "I am in a new space
which requires a new energy."
Allow the energy from that affirmation
to flow into you.

Date ___________

Daily Journal

Date _____________

____

*Knowing is only half the battle. You have
to put action behind that awareness.*

Daily Journal

Date __________

Daily Journal

Date __________

You have always been good enough.

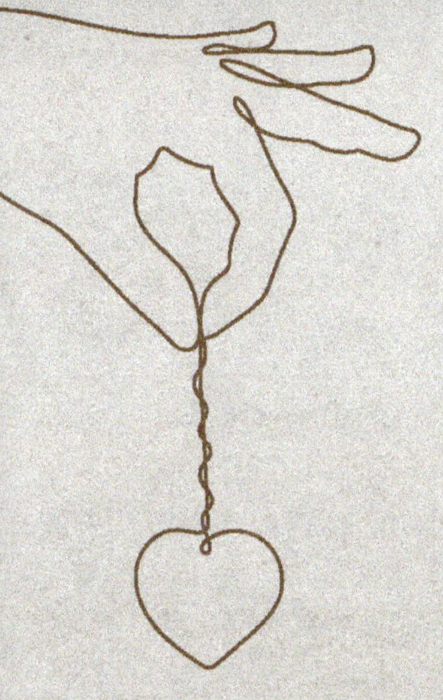

Human connection is beautiful, but you need emotional balance so you don't start feeling disconnected from yourself. A space where you can be heard, honest, held, and affirmed. Creating the balance is a mutual endeavor. Do people see you as clearly as you see them.

Daily Journal

Date ______________

Daily Journal

Date ______________

Once you realize you're falling back into old patterns, take some time to breathe. Give grace to yourself. Acknowledge without shame. Then make your pivot.

Daily Journal

Date ___________

Daily Journal

Date ______________

Dare to desire more than what you believe you deserve. See yourself in that place. It's okay to want more for yourself.

Daily Journal

Date ______________

Daily Journal

Date ___________

Daily Journal

Date ______________

What was your childhood like?
Then describe your happiest day in
childhood. Write about a change
that makes your life better.

In case you need to hear this.

Choose the new life that's choosing you. It's safe to let go of everything that isn't working. It's safe to let go now and trust that you're going in the right direction.

The greatest asset you have is your heart, your integrity. How you treat people - how your energy affects a place. You can be a rose or a thorn, the choice is your daily.

Deep breaths. You are surrounded by angels and love right now. Keep trusting, keep resting, keep affirming your boundaries.

Daily Journal

Date _______________

Reminder: The right people energize your spirit.

Daily Journal

Date ____________

Daily Journal

Date __________

In life there is always going to be risk -it's about finding the people that are worth it.

New beginnings.
Bigger leaps.
More heart expansion.
Deeper lover.
Deeper trust.
Less rushing through the process.
Letting time do its thing.

Daily Journal

Date __________

*Life gets sweeter. Keep trusting the process
and making your way to the safety and
safe relationships that you deserve.*

Daily Journal

Date _____________

Daily Journal

Date ___________

It's time to kill the idea that we can only grow and heal when we're uncomfortable. You heal every time you have a good conversation with someone. You heal every time you laugh. You heal every time something makes you smile genuinely. You heal every time you have fun creating something - anything. You heal every time you get so absorbed in something fun that you forget your struggles for a while. There is, in fact, lots of healing and growth to be found INSIDE your comfort zone.

Daily Journal

Date ___________

Don't forget to look around and appreciate the things that are going right as well.

Daily Journal

Date _____________

Daily Journal

Date _______________

Daily Journal

Date ____________

Things could have been different....
But who knows if they would have
been better?

Daily Journal

Date __________

Daily Journal

Date ___________

There was a whole you before them,
there will be a whole you after them.

Daily Journal

Date ______________

What's your biggest insecurity?
What would life look like if you let
it go?

In case you need to hear this.

You should be incredibly proud of how you've handled yourself and how hard you've worked on recovering from things you kept to yourself.

So much has grown you, so who you are becoming deserves celebration, but you've withstood so much that could've broke you, so who you are currently deserves applause too.

Daily Journal

Date ___________

Daily Journal

Date ___________

Focus more on being your own source of happiness, first.

Daily Journal

Date ___________

Reminder

You become the best version of yourself when you work on things that people can't take away from you. Work on your mindset, character, personality, transparency, and communication. That's the real upgrade.

Daily Journal

Date ___________

Daily Journal

Date ___________

*Let love meet you where you're at,
then lean into it.*

Daily Journal

Date _____________

Daily Journal

Date _____________

I know you're tired, but keep going.
Keep trying.

Daily Journal

Date ___________

Consider your current age and write down three things you love about this time in your life. Then think about your future self and think about what you would miss in your current life.

In case you need to hear this.

You have to learn to forgive yourself. The mistake didn't change your purpose. Don't let failures and times you got off course cause you to be against yourself. Be as merciful to yourself as you are to others.

Life changes. You lose love. You lose friends. you lose pieces of yourself that you never imagined would be gone. And then, without even realizing it, these pieces come back. New life enters. Better friends come along. And a stronger, wiser you is staring back in the mirror.

Your soul is always communicating with you. It tells you where it wants to go by making you aware of your interests. your desires, and what feels good to you. Follow your passions. When something stops bringing you joy, stop doing it. Shift and flow like the water.

Daily Journal

Date ____________

Daily Journal

Date ___________

Keep answering what's calling your soul.

Daily Journal

Date ___________

Daily Journal

Date ___________

Trust that what belongs to you will
always find you.

Daily Journal

Date ___________

Daily Journal

Date ___________

Daily Journal   Date ______________

Breathe. Everything you're going through right now is exactly what you need. Be calm, and embrace the journey. You're in the process of becoming the ultimate version of you.

Date _____________

In case you forgot, I'm proud of you.

Daily Journal

Date ______________

Daily Journal

Date __________

Breathe. You haven't met all of you yet.
There is so much more life left to live.

What are you looking for in a romantic relationship? How can you give it to yourself?

You survived multiple seasons where
you managed one crisis after the
next. May those experiences, and the
wisdom gained from them, help lay
the foundational support that leads
you to everything that is for you.
May this be the season where
everything starts aligning for you.

Daily Journal

Date ___________

You will be okay, love. You have always found a way to keep giving. This time won't be any different.

Daily Journal

Date ________

Daily Journal

Date ______________

Daily Journal

Date _____________

When you choose to forgive those who hurt you, you take away their power.

Daily Journal

Date _______________

When you come out on the other side of a karmic lesson with a deeper understanding. When you're giving yourself more compassion and can name what you're experiencing while processing all the moving parts of the lesson. That's still growth. Being able to identify and examine your triggers while moving through a lesson is still growth. You're growing and you're allowed to keep outgrowing your old programming while moving forward to safer and calmer waters.

Daily Journal

Date _______________

Date _______________

Daily Journal

Date _____________

You have to establish a new standard for yourself. You have to declare that you deserve a better quality of relationships and stand on that. You have to be unwavering, when those connections start showing up, you have to operate authentically and unselfishly within them.

Daily Journal

You deserve everything you desire.

Daily Journal

Date ___________

I know that one day, when you are finally in the place you have dreamt of, you will look back at this period of your life and feel so grateful that you did not give up.

Daily Journal

Date _______________

*I hope something good happens
for you today.*

Daily Journal

Date ___________

In case you need to hear this.

The simplest way to stop yourself from falling back
into old cycles and habits when you move to
a new space is telling yourself "I am in a new space
which requires a new energy." Allow the energy from
that affirmation to flow into you.

You don't have to remain the same person
everyone has always known you as. You don'thave
to remain the same person you have always known
yourself as. Keep stepping into your authentic self.

I know that one day, when you're finally in the
place you have dreamt of, you will look back at this
period of your life and feel so appreciative that
you held on and didn't give up.

When you're healing your avoidant
attachment style and becoming more
expressive and emotionally honest. It takes
time to recalibrate, align with the right
people, and start creating emotional balance
in your connections. It doesn't happen
overnight.

Daily Journal

Date _______________

Daily Journal

Date _______________

Daily Journal

Date ______________

When you come out on the other side of a karmic lesson with a deeper understanding. When you're giving yourself more compassion and can name what you're experiencing while processing all the moving parts of the lesson. That's still growth. You're growing and you're allowed to keep outgrowing your old programming while moving forward to safer and calmer waters.

Daily Journal

Date ___________

Date ___________

Date _______________

Sometimes taking a step back, to develop more clarity, is just as necessary as moving forward.

Daily Journal

Date _______________

Embrace your softness.
Embrace your vulnerability.
Don't let the world harden you.

Daily Journal

Date ______________

*I hope you win the war you
tell no one about.*

Motivation moves you forward, but what are you moving away from? What do you try your best to avoid in life? Are there certain emotions attached to these things that you don't want to experience?

In case you need to hear this.

Be grateful that certain things didn't work out. Sometimes you don't even realize what you're being protected from or where you're being guided to when you're in the midst of chaos. Trust that other things are aligning for you. Let go gracefully.

Sometimes you have to realize you can't talk it out with everybody. Some people are stuck in their ways, stubborn, and there's nothing you can say or do except remove yourself from the situation that's disturbing your peace. Stop holding onto a rope that's tearing your hand apart.

It's okay to feel sad while you grow at the same time. Feeling the things that you have to feel in order to get to the next step and doing the proper internal work is so important - it's the only way to truly heal your traumas, you can't get stuck on something forever and not do the work.

Date ______________

Daily Journal

Date _____________

Still love yourself while you are becoming the person you want to be.

Daily Journal

Date ______________

Repeat after me: Because I'm loved, I don't need to worry. Because I'm protected, I don't need to worry.

Daily Journal

Date ___________

Daily Journal

Date ______________

There may be some seasons where you have to go without, but you will never forget what those seasons taught you. You move way different after that.

Daily Journal

Date _______________

Daily Journal

Date ___________

*What a gift it is to return
back to yourself. Do it as
many times as you need to be.*

What are some mental health
practice that you can do now that
your future self will benefit from?

Free yourself from
unrealistic expectations.
Free yourself from goals
motivated by ego and pride.
Free yourself from the need
to be impressive. Define
success on your own terms
and watch how fast your
life changes.

Date __________

Daily Journal

Date ___________

I hope you find a soft place to land soon.

Daily Journal

Date ______________

It's okay to change your mind. It's okay to grow and recognize you're too deeply loved to settle for what some people tried to offer you. Change your mind, it's okay.

Daily Journal

Date ___________

159

As you begin to decide what you want to do with life. Please do everything with love. Commit to releasing everything less than love. Commit to loving yourself properly with your nutrition choices, sleep patterns, and the relationships that you are choosing. There is a deep love that is flowing through your soul. I hope you tap into that love every day, and I hope you select choices that add to your vitality. You are already free - you are love.

Daily Journal

Date __________

*Don't shrink yourself.
It's okay to outgrow
people who once had the
chance to grow with you.*

Daily Journal

Date ___________

*You deserve all the good things
that are happening for you
and you deserve all of the good
things that are coming.*

Date _____________

Daily Journal   Date ______________

I'm proud of you for not giving up on yourself. I'm so glad you made it this far.

Now go over everything you wrote in this journal and do some reflecting. Is there something you want to change? How do you feel? What are your goals moving forward?

Repeat after me:
I am flourishing.
I am worthy of greatness.
I accept myself as I am.
I can do anything
I trust myself.
I am enough.
I am whole.
I am never a burden.
The world is a better place with me in it.
I am proud of myself and all that I have
accomplished. My potential to succeed is infinite.

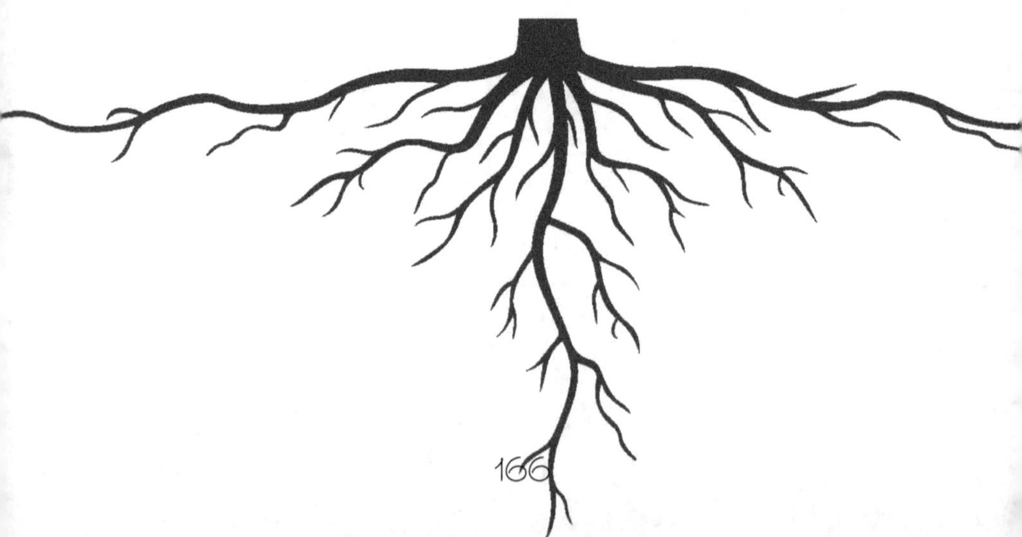

I hope you slowly bloom into the person you truly want to be. Remember to always take it one day at a time, enjoy the process, and stay present in the moment. Now go water yourself and bloom.

Annie Giang

167

ABOUT THE AUTHOR

Annie Giang was born in Vietnam, but has called the U.S home since she was just a couple months old. She fosters a deep appreciation for diverse traditions and experiences as an enthusiastic traveler because her childhood was shaped by rich blend of cultures.

While navigating challenges during her junior year of college, Annie received heartbreaking news about her grandmother's passing the day before her final exam, concealed by her mom until later. She completely lost it. This devastating news led her into a tumultuous period of drinking and drugs. A few months after her grandmother's passing, a call from her brother marked a transformative shift as she learned she was to become an aunt, infusing a newfound sense of purpose. This prompted her to seek therapy and embrace fitness for self-discovery, reigniting her passion for writing and journaling. By expressing her feelings and reflections in writing, she discovered a deeper meaning to life, finding clarity and peace. This is where she rediscovered herself.

After relocating to the Houston area, her current residence, she embarked on a self-love journey. It was during moments of solitude and self-discovery that she penned this journal. With a newly gained lens of self-awareness, Annie hoped to publish a journal that would assist those in similarly difficult situations on how to navigate their feelings.

* 9 7 9 8 2 1 8 3 6 9 1 3 2 *